# THE GREAT COMMUNICATOR

## THE LIFE OF PRESIDENT RONALD REAGAN

US History Book Presidents Grade 3
Children's American History

Speedy Publishing LLC
40 E. Main St. #1156
Newark, DE 19711
www.speedypublishing.com

Ronald Reagan was a well-known actor, and went on to become an admired politician. Read about how his life took him from movie studios right to the White House!

Photograph of Ronald Reagan
(with "Dutch boy" haircut)

# YOUNG RONALD REAGAN

Ronald Reagan was born in Illinois in 1911. The family was not well off, and lived when Reagan was small in an apartment without running water. Reagan's father called him "Dutch" when he was a baby, thinking his round face made him look like a fat Dutch businessman. The nickname stuck with him for the rest of his life.

The family finally settled in Dixon, Illinois, west of Chicago. Reagan was an athlete and the president of the student body at the Dixon high school, and acted in school plays. In the summers, he worked as a lifeguard.

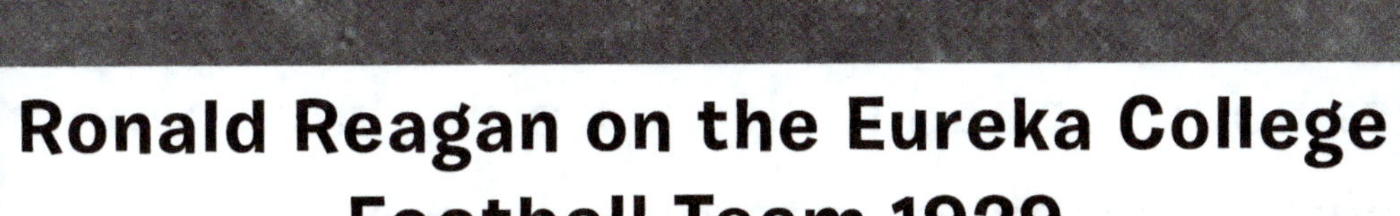

Ronald Reagan on the Eureka College Football Team 1929

Reagan went to Eureka College, not far from Dixon. He was a multi-sport athlete, acted in plays, and was president of the student government.

# A PERFORMER

After college, Reagan went to work as a sports announcer on for a radio station in Iowa. In those days the reports of the game arrived on a "ticker tape", with just the highlights: "Jones hits a single to right." The announcer had to dress up the bare report into a colorful story for the radio audience: "And here's the pitch, a slider.

Ronald Reagan as Radio Announcer

Jones swings desperately at the last moment! He just gets the end of the bat on the ball. But look at that! It loops over the leaping second baseman and drops in for a hit, the first hit of the series for Jones. He's at first base now, a happy grin on his face." Reagan was very good at story-telling!

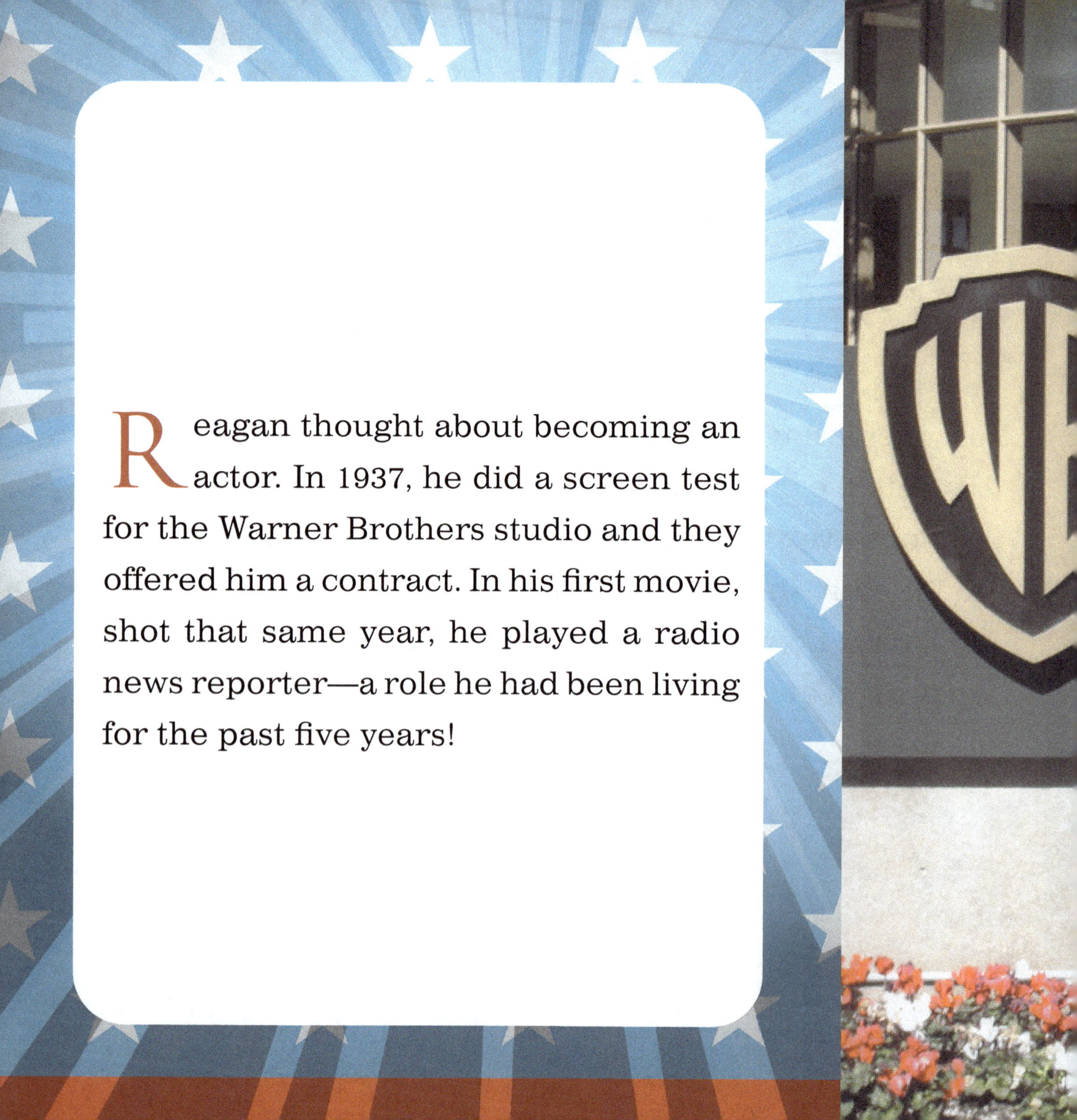

Reagan thought about becoming an actor. In 1937, he did a screen test for the Warner Brothers studio and they offered him a contract. In his first movie, shot that same year, he played a radio news reporter—a role he had been living for the past five years!

WARNER BROS. STUDIOS

A photo from the movie "The Killers"

Between then and 1964, Ronald Reagan appeared in more than 50 movies. He was never a super-star, but he was a reliable actor who often played the leading man's best friend. He only played a bad guy once, in his very last film, The Killers.

During World War II, from 1941 to 1945, a lot of actors left Hollywood to join the army, navy, or air force. Reagan joined the army, but could not go into combat because his eyesight was poor. Instead, he stayed in California and made training films for the Army.

Reagan married twice, both times to actresses. His second wife, Nancy Davis, married him in 1952 and they stayed married until his death.

For six years Ronald Reagan was president of the Screen Actors Guild. During that time he testified before a committee of Congress about the presence of communists in the film industry. To find out more about this philosophy, read the Baby Professor book What is Communism?

Ronald and Nancy Reagan

Reagan had been a Democrat, and supported the policies of President Roosevelt in the 1930s and 1940s. However, after the war his thinking became more and more conservative.

He spent eight years as a spokesman for the General Electric Company, and was often called on to make speeches complaining about government regulations and interference in business development.

**ELECTRIC APPLIANCES.** Mrs. Stanley Johnson, Arlington Heights, Ill.: "I just love our Medallion home – especially the kitchen. All these electric appliances that came with it – like this wall oven – sure make my job much easier. And my husband says they're easier to buy this way, because we pay for them on the mortgage."

178

# buyers – the Live Better Electrically MEDALLION

This new Medallion assures you a home has been inspected by the local electric utility... meets modern standards for wiring, appliances and lighting. Look for the Medallion. It means a wonderful new way of life for you and your family!

Ronald Reagan
GENERAL ELECTRIC

**What Sterling is to silver... that's what this Medallion is to a new house! It's the new national symbol of the finest in electrical living. Let these three top TV stars, speaking here for the electrical industry, tell how you save trouble, time, and money by choosing a home that wears the Live Better Electrically Medallion.**

**BETTY:** In a Medallion home, you start right off with a modern electric range, plus at least 3 additional major appliances, maybe more. They're installed, ready to go to work the day you move in! Appliances are easier to pay for this way.

**RONNIE:** The lighting in every Medallion home is specially planned, too. It provides better light for better sight, plus new beauty for your home. You also get full Housepower. This means enough power, wiring, circuits, switches, and outlets to handle all the appliances you want to use.

**FRAN:** You'll be glad all your life you bought a Medallion home. Read below what a few of the thousands of new Medal lion home owners think o them. Then go see the Medal lion homes in your neighbor hood. Your electric utility wil tell you where they are.

**New Ideas for Better Living**

The new Medallion is backe up by home builders, electri utilities, and electrical manu facturers (Frigidaire, Genera Electric, Hotpoint, Kelvinator Thermador, Westinghouse Whirlpool, and others). Thi year, utilities will award Me dallions to 100,000 new home —in every style and price rang across the country. You'll se lots of new ideas in the Medal lion homes on display now!

## UL FEATURES LIKE THESE IN MEDALLION HOMES!

Live Better Electrically Ad

G. Mr. and Mrs. Charles R. McCarty, Greensboro, r knew you could do so many beautiful things with bought a Medallion home. Valance lighting, for ur furniture and drapes look wonderful – and at the ur son a well-lighted place to practice the piano."

BETTER HOMES & GARDENS, OCTOBER, 195

FULL ... the things I like most in my Medallion home is all the handy outlets. I can plug in my portable cooking appliances wherever I want and use them – even with the washer going – without ever blowing a fuse. And I can cook a meal anywhere in the house – and outdoors, too."

BETTER HOMES & GARDENS, OCTOBER, 1958

...re electric heating, too. These are awarded a special Gold Medallion. The all-electric heat pump, shown here in the home of Mr. and Mrs. William Isaac of Beverly Hills, California, provides year-round comfort from a single unit which automatically heats or cools as the weather requires.

179

TO THE HEROIC
D2RN E2RN
OF THE
WHO UNDER THE
COLONEL JAMES E
THE FIRST AMERICAN
AND TOOK
THE POINTE

# A POLITICIAN

In the 1960s, Ronald Reagan began to move toward running for public office. He supported Barry Goldwater in his failed run for president in 1964 and became a regular speaker at political events.

Photograph of Governor Ronald and family

In 1966 Reagan ran for office for the first time, and was elected as governor of California. He was re-elected in 1970.

Learn more about elections in the United States in the Baby Professor book Everything You Need to Know about the US Voting System.

# PRESIDENT REAGAN

Ronald Reagan tried to become the Republican candidate for president in 1968 and in 1976, but both times other men were chosen. Finally, he was nominated by the Republicans for the 1980 election. Reagan and running mate George H. W. Bush defeated President Jimmy Carter and his Vice President, Walter Mondale. He was 69 years old, and the oldest person to have been elected president.

George H. W. Bush

President Ronald Reagan

Ronald Reagan became president in January, 1981, during an economic crisis. In his first address, he said that government action was not the solution to the economic problems; in fact, government was itself the problem!

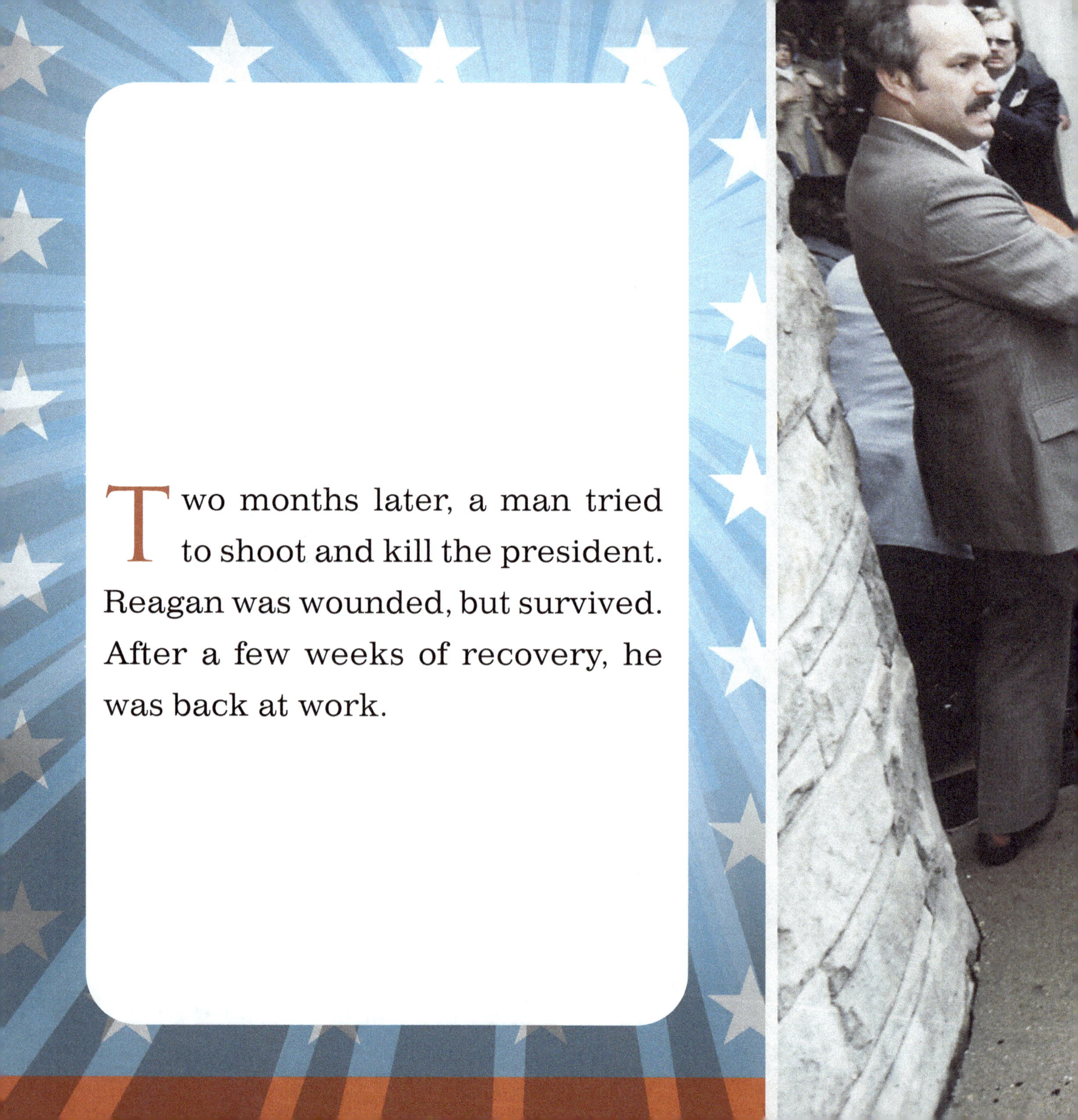

Two months later, a man tried to shoot and kill the president. Reagan was wounded, but survived. After a few weeks of recovery, he was back at work.

Chaos outside the Washington Hilton Hotel after the assassination attempt on President Reagan

# DOMESTIC POLICIES

As president, Ronald Reagan pushed to reduce the influence of government in the business of the United States. He wanted to reduce regulations and cut taxes. He believed that tax cuts would pay for themselves, because increasing the amount of money in people's pockets would increase economic activity. At the same time he pushed for increased spending on the military and reducing spending on programs to help people in economic need.

Reagan cut taxes so deeply that it caused serious problems for the government. He raised taxes as often as he cut them, in an attempt to find the right balance of low taxes and sufficient government revenue. During his time in office the national debt (the amount of money the government has borrowed and will one day have to pay back) grew dramatically.

President Reagan giving the State of the Union Address

President Reagan and His Supreme Court Justice Nominee Sandra Day O'Connor

In 1981, Reagan appointed Sandra Day O'Connor to the United States Supreme Court. She was the first woman to have a seat on the highest court in the nation.

# FOREIGN AFFAIRS

Under Reagan, the United States military expanded greatly. Pressure and tension increased in the conflict for dominance between the United States and the Soviet Union that was known as the "Cold War". The United States provided aid around the world to movements struggling to overthrow governments aligned with the Soviet Union.

COLD
W★R

The United States also got more involved in the Middle East, attempting to keep the peace between Israel, the world's only Jewish state, and the Arab nations on all sides of it.

**Israel Defense Forces - US-Israel Military Cooperation**

## US Army in Lebanon

Over 200 United States Marines were killed in Lebanon when suicide bombers blew up their barracks.

In his second term Ronald Reagan was able to make a more creative relationship with the new leader of the Soviet Union, Mikhail Gorbachev. In 1987 the two countries signed an agreement to get rid of a large number of nuclear weapons. Reagan challenged Gorbachev to tear down the Berlin Wall, a symbol of the division between the Soviet Bloc and western countries. Learn more about this, and how the Wall finally came down, in the Baby Professor book Who Built the Berlin Wall?

Mikhail Gorbachev and Ronald Reagan

President Reagan was re-elected in a landslide victory in 1984 over Walter Mondale and his vice-presidential running mate, Geraldine Ferraro. However, his reputation became clouded by a series of scandals involving many members of his government. In particular, high officials were charged with involvement in what became known as "Iran-Contra", in which officials violated United States law by trading with Iran to gain money with which to support a Central American struggle against a left-wing government.

Garden of Ronald Reagan
Presidential Library and Museum

# LATER YEARS

Ronald and Nancy Reagan left Washington in January, 1989 as George H. W. Bush became president. The Reagans returned to California and Reagan worked on plans for the Ronald Reagan Presidential Library and Museum. The site opened in 1991.

In 1994, Reagan revealed that he had Alzheimer's disease, an ailment that affects memory and reasoning ability. He had to deal with the disease for the next ten years, until he died at age 93 in 2004.

President Ronald Reagan's horse-drawn casket is saluted by a U.S. Coast Guardsman

Ronald Reagan led a rise of conservative policies in the United States and a move toward smaller government and lower tax rates. He is revered by some as the patron saint of small government and a muscular foreign policy by the United States, while others criticize him for running the country into debt and hurting the poor in order to benefit the rich.

# RONALD REAGAN FACTS

Reagan's favorite snack was jelly beans, and his favorite flavor was licorice. He started eating them in 1967 as he tried to quit smoking.

A food he really did not like was Brussels sprouts. He was not fond of tomatoes, either, but he ate a lot of them in the course of his political career, as he attended many banquets.

**Jelly beans**

In one of his movies, Reagan was near a gun that was fired. The sound permanently damaged his hearing in one ear.

Ronald Reagan was the first person who had been divorced to become president. Donald Trump, elected in 2016, is the only other United States president to have been divorced.

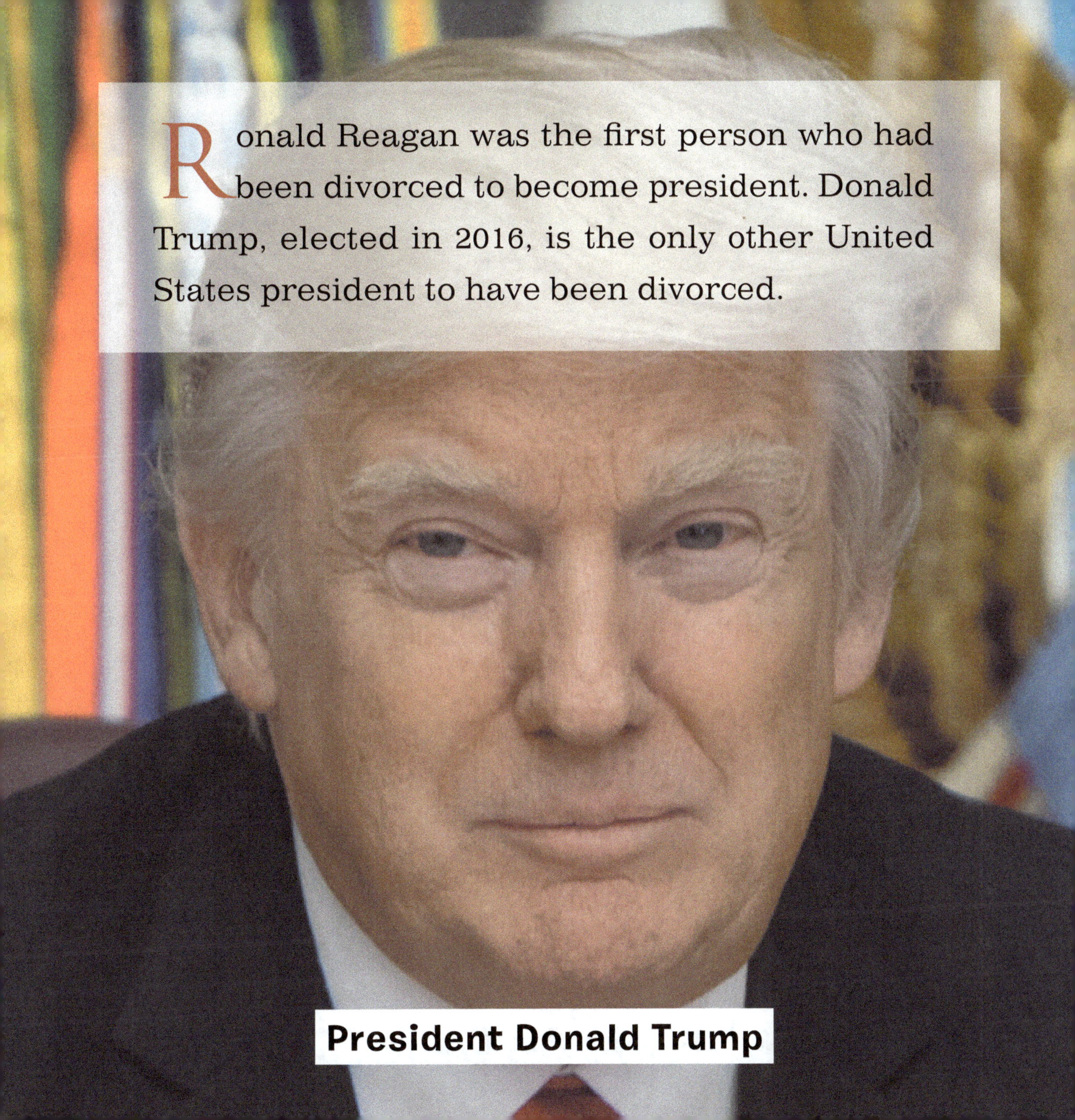

President Donald Trump

Reagan was an athlete in many sports in his high-school and college days in Illinois, but perhaps his most important athletic effort was as a lifeguard. During his summers at beaches and pools, Reagan saved as many as 80 people from drowning.

Ronal Raegan as Life Guard

# COULD YOU BE A POLITICIAN?

Many of the best politicians bring experience in other fields to their work in elected office. Some, like George Washington, Ulysses S. Grant, and Dwight Eisenhower, had been generals. Others, like Woodrow Wilson and Barack Obama, were college professors. Becoming good at a career you like helps you succeed in that career, and it may even prepare you for elected office.

Learn more about what that involves in the Baby Professor book How Does the US Government Work?

Visit

www.BabyProfessorBooks.com

to download Free Baby Professor eBooks and view our catalog of new and exciting Children's Books

www.ingramcontent.com/pod-product-compliance
Lightning Source LLC
LaVergne TN
LVHW060828170826
845678LV00010B/1928

* 9 7 9 8 8 6 9 4 3 2 1 9 3 *